Celebrating Chinese New Year

Diane Hoyt-Goldsmith

Photographs by Lawrence Migdale

Holiday House / New York

This book is dedicated
to the memory of
Uncle Wes
November 30, 1942 – October 11, 1997

Library of Congress Cataloging-in-Publication Data
Hoyt-Goldsmith, Diane.
    Celebrating Chinese New Year / Diane Hoyt-Goldsmith ; photographs
by Lawrence Migdale.
        p.   cm.
    Summary: Depicts a San Francisco boy and his family preparing for
and enjoying their celebration of the Chinese New Year, their most
important holdiay.
    ISBN 0-8234-1393-4 (reinforced)
    1. Chinese New Year — Juvenile literature. [1. Chinese New Year.
2. Holidays.] I. Title.
GT4905.H68   1998
394.261 — dc21
                                            98-17028
                                            CIP
                                                    AC

Acknowledgments
We would like to thank Raymond and Karen Leong and their children, Kristi and Ryan, for sharing their Chinese New Year celebration with us. We are also grateful to their entire extended family, especially to Grandma Sue (Susan Lum) and all the aunts and uncles and cousins for their support and cooperation.

Also, we thank the principal of the Alamo School in San Francisco, Mrs. Dobbie Quinones, and the teachers at Ryan's Chinese school, Mrs. Jane Kwan and Mrs. Ivy De Luz.

We appreciate the help of many other individuals and groups: Gayle Gin of Hair Today Beauty Salon in San Francisco, Joette Langianese of On Lok Senior Health Center, Danny Chang of the United Savings Bank in Chinatown, and Jasmine Tuan of the Chinese Historical Society of America.

Alex Lee and all the members of the Leung Brothers White Crane Kung Fu Association were very cooperative in allowing us to photograph the Lion Dance on location in Chinatown. A special thank-you to the late Thomas Chinn, whose friendship and guidance were instrumental in beginning this story of the Chinese New Year in San Francisco. We appreciate the helpful comments of David Lei and his special insights into Chinese culture and tradition and their meaning for contemporary Chinese American children.

For more information about the Chinese New Year's Parade in San Francisco, please contact:
Chinese New Year Festival and Parade
809 Montgomery Street
San Francisco, CA 94133
You can also experience the Chinese New Year Parade on the World Wide Web at:
    http://www.channelA.com

Gung hay fat choy is a traditional Chinese New Year's greeting that means "May you prosper." Ryan can hardly wait to hear it. He and his family are getting ready to celebrate Chinese New Year, the most important holiday of the year. His family will gather together to show their love and support for one another. They will visit friends and family and honor their ancestors. Ryan and other children will receive gifts, and everyone will celebrate in special ways.

Getting Ready for the New Year

Chinese New Year has been celebrated for more than four thousand years. Dating from 2697 B.C.E., it grew out of ancient celebrations marking the end of winter and the beginning of spring.

The date of the celebration is determined by the Chinese lunar calendar. This system of measuring time is based upon the moon and its cycles. Each month begins with a new moon and has either twenty-nine or thirty days. That is why the Chinese New Year is also called the Lunar New Year.

The Chinese New Year celebration lasts for fifteen days. It begins with New Year's Eve on the second new moon after the winter solstice and ends with the Lantern Festival held at the full moon two weeks later. According to the Gregorian calendar that is used in the United States, the Chinese New Year falls between late January and late February, but the exact date varies from year to year.

A week or so before the New Year, Ryan and his family start to prepare for it. First of all, they clean the house from top to bottom. They sweep the dust and dirt out the door along with all the bad luck that has collected in the house. People buy new clothes or a new pair of shoes to get ready and everyone tries to pay all of their debts for a fresh start.

Ryan lives in San Francisco with his mother and father and an older sister named Kristi. San Francisco has one of the largest Chinese populations of any city in the United States. About twenty percent of all the people who live in San Francisco are Chinese or Chinese American.

Ryan and his sister, Kristi, "sweep away" the old to symbolize their readiness for all the things that the New Year will bring.

In the 1850s, many Chinese people immigrated to the United States to look for gold during the California gold rush. Historians estimate that in 1851, one in every ten people in California was Chinese. Later, Chinese immigrants provided services to the miners, working as cooks and opening laundries. In the 1860s, Chinese engineering skill and experience helped build the railroads that soon crossed the nation from coast to coast.

(Below) Before the New Year, Ryan gets a haircut. The Chinese word for hair sounds like the word for prosperity. People do not want to cut their prosperity, or their hair, just as the New Year is beginning.

(Above) Ryan's mother puts away all the knives so that they won't accidentally "cut their luck" in the New Year. Many Chinese families follow ancient traditions like these because they are symbolic links to their ancestors and the past.

Chinatown streets are crowded as shoppers buy the things they need for the New Year celebration.

Today there are several neighborhoods in San Francisco where large numbers of Chinese people live and work. One of the oldest and largest of these is called Chinatown.

Just before New Year begins, Chinatown is even more crowded than usual. Chinese people come from all over the city to buy flowers and other necessities for the New Year. For the Chinese, plants and flowers are symbols of rebirth, because without the flower, a plant cannot make seeds or bear fruit.

(Right) The Flower Festival is an outdoor market in Chinatown with beautiful flowers for sale. Peach and quince blossoms, with buds just ready to open, are a popular choice. People say that if the buds open on New Year's Day, it will bring a year of good luck and prosperity.

(Left) Ryan's mother hires a calligrapher to write a poem for their home. Ryan and his grandmother watch as the man paints a poetic saying. These sayings, written on bright red paper, give the home a festive atmosphere during the New Year.

The Chinese word for "orange" sounds very close to the sound of the word for "gold." For that reason, oranges are thought to bring good fortune.

Ryan and his father select oranges to place on their family altar and to bring as gifts to their friends on New Year's Day. Oranges represent money and wealth, while tangerines are symbols of good luck. People believe that displaying both fruits will bring good luck and prosperity in the year ahead.

As Ryan and his father shop in Chinatown, people are especially polite and helpful. They believe that their good behavior will insure luck and prosperity in the year to come.

This stationery store in Chinatown has a large selection of gift envelopes called lai see. Red is the color of happiness for the Chinese. These envelopes, with a gift of money inside, are given to children on Chinese New Year.

Ryan's father selects some dried scallops for the New Year's soup.

Ryan's Shopping List
(with the symbolic meanings for some items)

Oranges / gold

Tangerines with leaves / good luck

Ginkgo Nuts / unity

Dried Oysters / successful business

Fat Choy / prosperity — a black, mosslike seaweed

Lotus Root / continuous sons

Whole Fresh Fish / surplus

Whole Fresh Chicken / good future

Lettuce / to grow or spread prosperity
The Chinese word for "lettuce" sounds like the word for "birth," so lettuce represents the birth of the New Year.

Shark's Fin / A small piece, just a few inches long, is very rare and can cost more than a hundred dollars. This is an ingredient for a special New Year's soup.

Honoring Ancestors

This photograph, taken in China, shows Ryan's grandparents when they were young. His grandfather Willie was the first Asian American to receive a Purple Heart for bravery during World War I. His grandmother Wai Chow Chan came to California on a crowded freighter. After she married Willie, they worked in a cannery, cutting beans. Sometimes she shelled shrimp, earning ten cents a pound for her labor. She also sewed pockets on jeans for just twenty-five cents a dozen. Ryan's grandparents both worked hard to succeed in the United States.

One of the most important parts of celebrating the New Year is honoring ancestors. This means both the elderly relatives still living, as well as those who have died. Before the New Year begins, Ryan goes to the cemetery with his father to clean the stone that marks the place where his grandmother and grandfather are buried. This is a solemn time for Ryan and his father.

This tradition comes from China of long ago when most people lived in rural villages. Care for the elderly was an obligation that each child learned early in life. It was an important responsibility. As a result, people grew up with strong feelings of belonging to a family and a community.

Ryan helps his father wash the stone on his grandparents' grave.

After cleaning the stone, Ryan and his father place oranges and fresh flowers there as an offering. He and his father say a prayer for their relatives, who are lovingly remembered.

At Chinese School

*T*en-year-old Ryan is in the fourth grade at Alamo School in San Francisco. In addition to his regular school, Ryan is enrolled in a program to learn about Chinese language and culture. He attends Chinese school for an hour after each school day.

Ryan started Chinese school in first grade, so he has been attending for four years. Already he has learned to read and write in Chinese. Although both of Ryan's parents speak the Cantonese dialect of Chinese, they speak English at home. Ryan is shy about speaking Chinese, but he gets more confident every day.

His teachers, Mrs. Kwan and Mrs. De Luz, show the children how to write New Year's messages on bright red paper. The students write the messages with a soft brush that they dip into black ink. When Ryan writes, he paints a Chinese character to represent each word in the message. It takes a lot of practice to write a Chinese character with a brush. It is a little like painting a picture. This special way of writing is called calligraphy.

Ryan writes two poems in Chinese characters. They are called fai chun and often consist of four characters. These are familiar sayings in Chinese that everyone knows, such as "Gung hay fat choy." The one he is just finishing means "Wealth will come and always improve." The one to his left means "Good luck and lots of profit." Ryan will decorate his house with these for the New Year.

Mrs. Kwan shows Ryan how to hold the brush properly. The children are encouraged to write the Chinese characters over and over again. This helps the students to remember them. It takes great discipline and many years of study to learn to read and write in Chinese. For this reason, education is highly valued.

The Animals of the Chinese Zodiac

*T*he Chinese Calendar counts years by groups of sixty. Each of these periods has cycles of twelve years with each determined by one of five elements: wood, fire, air, water, or earth. Each year is named after an animal. In addition, each two-hour period in the day is governed by an animal. For example, the hours from 11 PM until 1 AM are governed by the Rat, from 1 AM until 3 AM by the Ox, and so on. The characteristics of each animal are said to determine the way that people born at a certain time in a certain year will act.

Long ago, Buddha was said to have called all the animals on earth. Only twelve animals came: the rat, the ox, the tiger, the rabbit, the dragon, the snake, the horse, the sheep, the monkey, the rooster, the dog, and the pig. As a reward, Buddha gave each animal a year in the cycle and declared that anyone born in that year would resemble the animal in some way.

In China, individual birth dates are not as important as the year in which a person is born. Everyone, no matter which month they were born in, turns another year older on the seventh day of the New Year's celebration. In China, this is called People's Day or the Day of Man.

The order of the years in the Chinese calendar is Rat, Ox, Tiger, Rabbit, Dragon, Snake, Horse, Sheep, Monkey, Rooster, Dog, and Pig. Then the twelve-year cycle starts over again with the Rat. The symbol in the center of the wheel stands for yin and yang, the harmony of opposites.

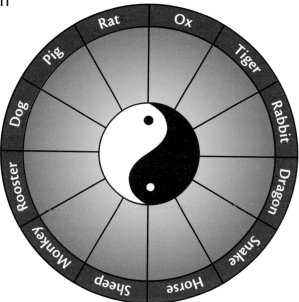

Rat

Feb. 10, 1948

Jan. 28, 1960

Feb. 15, 1972

Feb. 2, 1984

Feb. 19, 1996

Charming, creative, ambitious, friendly

Ox

Jan. 29, 1949

Feb. 15, 1961

Feb. 3, 1973

Feb. 20, 1985

Feb. 7, 1997

Steadfast, loyal, dependable, honest, strong

Tiger

Feb. 17, 1950

Feb. 5, 1962

Jan. 23, 1974

Feb. 9, 1986

Jan. 28, 1998

Brave, warm, impetuous, sincere

Rabbit

Feb. 6, 1951
Jan. 25, 1963
Feb. 11, 1975
Jan. 29, 1987
Feb. 16, 1999

Aloof, shy, humble, quiet

Horse

Feb. 3, 1954
Jan. 21, 1966
Feb. 7, 1978
Jan. 27, 1990
Feb. 12, 2002

Competitive, cheerful,
talented, impatient

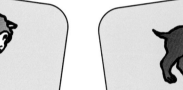

Rooster

Jan. 31, 1957
Feb. 17, 1969
Feb. 5, 1981
Jan. 23, 1993
Feb. 9, 2005

Determined, proud,
confident

Dragon

Jan. 27, 1952
Feb. 13, 1964
Jan. 31, 1976
Feb. 17, 1988
Feb. 5, 2000

Flamboyant, imaginative, strong,
decisive

Sheep

Jan. 24, 1955
Feb. 9, 1967
Jan. 28, 1979
Feb. 15, 1991
Feb. 1, 2003

Affectionate, trusting,
artistic, complacent

Dog

Feb. 18, 1958
Feb. 6, 1970
Jan. 25, 1982
Feb. 10, 1994
Jan. 29, 2006

Loyal, trustworthy, likable,
sympathetic

Snake

Feb. 14, 1953
Feb. 2, 1965
Feb. 18 1977
Feb. 6, 1989
Jan. 24, 2001

Restrained, subtle, tricky

Monkey

Feb. 12, 1956
Jan. 30, 1968
Feb. 16, 1980
Feb. 4, 1992
Jan. 22, 2004

Humorous, inventive,
mischievous

Pig

Feb. 8, 1959
Jan. 27, 1971
Feb. 13, 1983
Jan. 31, 1995
Feb. 18, 2007

Industrious, hardworking, caring

The First Day of the New Year

On the first day of the New Year, family and friends go visiting. They bring oranges, tangerines, and sweets as gifts. There is a Chinese tradition that if you haven't paid a visit to your relatives by the third day of the New Year, it is best not to go at all. That means that you won't get along for the rest of the year.

For Ryan's family, the best part of the Chinese New Year celebration is a big dinner for the entire family. Eating a meal together on New Year's Day shows the importance of family unity. Ryan's family invites all their relatives who live in San Francisco. Ryan's grandmother, aunts, uncles, and cousins will all be there. His parents, as hosts of the meal, plan an elaborate menu.

The New Year's feast takes many days to prepare. There is shopping for all the ingredients and then the careful preparation. Ryan's father, who is a professional chef, enjoys cooking traditional dishes. Ryan always likes to help.

All the food for New Year's Day is prepared before the New Year begins. The Chinese say that if a person works on New Year's Day, he will have to work that much harder all through the coming year.

Ryan's father plans a menu with many special New Year's dishes. He will serve chicken and duck. These will be cut up after cooking, but then put back together on the serving platter, including the heads and feet, to symbolize completeness and family unity. Eating these foods is said to help keep the family together.

On New Year's Eve Ryan's family eats a traditional meal called jai. This is a rich vegetarian dish influenced by the Buddhists. Some people believe that eating it purifies the body for the New Year.

16

The soup that starts the New Year meal is very special. It is made only for important occasions like this one. Using dried scallops, dried abalone, and a piece of dried shark's fin, the delicious soup will bring good health to all who eat it.

Ryan brings his father a plate of chee goo, a type of arrowroot, that is one of the foods eaten on New Year's.

Most Chinese dishes are made up of foods that are cut into bite-size pieces, then cooked at high heat in a pan called a wok. Many different vegetables and meats are put together in delicious combinations for each dish. A Chinese banquet usually consists of many separate courses, brought to the table one after another.

Ryan's family serves a New Year's meal made up of ten courses.

Ryan's Family's New Year's Menu

Shark's Fin Soup made from dried scallops, dried abalone, and dried shark's fin

Poached Chicken with head and feet

Peking Roast Duck with Nine-Layer Buns

Black Bean and Garlic Lobster Tails

Vegetarian Braised Vegetables including lotus root, pea pods, carrots cut to look like little fish, asparagus, and fresh water chestnuts

Sweet and Sour Shrimp

Diced Oyster Tumble Soong, six different vegetables cut into tiny squares, cooked with the oysters and served wrapped in a lettuce leaf.

Steamed Black Bass

Chee Goo with Ginger Dipping Sauce, a special vegetable eaten so as to have a son

Almond Gelatin with Tangerines and Raspberry Puree

(Above) Ryan and his family enjoy the New Year's feast. They eat at a round table, which is a symbol of unity. Ryan's family eats with chopsticks and each dish is placed in the center of the table to be shared with everyone.

(Right) Ryan shows honor to his grandmother by serving her a dumpling.

Ryan adds tangerines and oranges, a plate of sweets, and a large, yellow fruit called a pomelo to the family altar.

On New Year's Day, Ryan prepares the family altar. First he places pictures of his relatives who have died—his grandmother and grand-father—on a low table. He hangs the sayings he wrote in Chinese school on the wall.

Things for Ryan to Do on Chinese New Year's

(Above) Ryan gives his grandmother oranges to bring wealth in the New Year.

(Above) Ryan decorates the front door of his family's home with a Chinese character called fook. This is a character that means "prosperity." When hung upside down, it means "luck has arrived."

(Right) Ryan's grandmother presents him with lai see. The front has a Happy New Year greeting on it. Inside is some money. Adults give lai see to children and unmarried adults.

The Lion Dance

The Lion Dance has been an important tradition in China since the late Han dynasty in about 100 A.D. Although in the beginning there were no lions in China, they were imported there from other parts of the world. Today Lion Dancers are active in Chinese communities all over the world. However, they are busiest during the celebration of the Chinese New Year.

Lion Dancers are young men and women who are members of martial arts clubs. They train together for many years to develop the skill, discipline, bravery, teamwork, and intelligence needed in their performances. Lion Dancing is good training for life because the same skills are needed to overcome life's obstacles.

Members of the White Crane Kung Fu Association gather to prepare for a Lion Dance performance during the New Year celebration in Chinatown.

During the Chinese New Year celebration, businesses invite the Lion Dancers to pay a visit. At the entrance to a bank or a shop, the Lion Dancers perform to the sound of drums. It takes two dancers working as a team to make one lion come to life. One dancer works the front of the lion and another dancer works the back. Using strings attached to the inside of the mask, the dancers can make the lion's ears wiggle, the eyes blink, the mouth open, and the tail wag. Dancers need strength, agility, teamwork, endurance, and balance to perform well.

The man in the pink mask represents a Buddhist monk and provides some comic relief. He holds up a fan to drive the lion back.

23

(Above) In front of a business, the Lion Dancers climb a pile of boxes to get to the goal, a bunch of lettuce and green onions that hang above the door.

(Left) When the Lion Dancer reaches the greens, he pretends to gobble them up along with the lai see that is attached. This part of the dance is symbolic of the need to overcome obstacles in life through intelligence, hardwork, and diligence.

24

More Fun for the New Year

(Below) Ryan's cousins help make cookies called dahn sahn for the New Year. They are made by twisting wonton wrappers into the shape of butterflies. Ryan's aunt fries them in oil. Then the children sprinkle the cookies with powdered sugar.

Long ago in China, cooking oil was scarce and expensive. For this reason, these cookies are a special treat made to celebrate the New Year.

(Above) One of Ryan's cousins is a Lion Dancer. He helps Ryan and some other cousins put on a parade in the backyard.

The Chinese New Year's Parade

In San Francisco, the final New Year celebration is the annual Chinese New Year's Parade. Since 1953, a parade has been held in San Francisco's Chinatown. Each year it seems to get bigger and better.

(Right) Children from San Francisco's Guadalupe School perform the Flower Drum Dance for the parade.

(Below) This float was made to celebrate the Lantern Festival that ends the Chinese New Year celebration.

(Above) Lion Dancers from the San Francisco police force perform.

(Right) Ryan and his sister admire some of the costumes worn during the parade.

The Chinese New Year's parade is an opportunity for the Chinese community to share its culture with the rest of the city. Just as it starts to get dark, the parade winds its way through downtown streets, with marching bands, martial arts clubs, civic leaders, beauty queens, Lion Dancers, and sinuous, fast-moving dragons.

The dragon, an animal from Chinese mythology, represents strength and brings good luck. Every Chinese New Year's parade ends with one. The dragon has the eyes of a rabbit, the mouth of a camel, the antlers of a deer, the scales of a carp, the whiskers of a catfish, the talons of an eagle, the legs of a tiger, the ears of a cow, and the body of a serpent.

As the dragon passes by, firecrackers explode all around. The old year ends with a roar as people celebrate the beginning of a new one.

恭喜發財

Gung hay fat choy!

May you prosper!

Ryan and Kristi open their lai see and count the money they have received as gifts from their friends and relatives.

The Chinese New Year celebration has given Ryan and his family a chance to renew friendships, think about loved ones who have died, and plan for the year ahead. Best of all, they have celebrated their Chinese heritage. Celebrating the Chinese New Year gives Ryan and his family the chance to experience a valuable link with the past as they look forward to the future.

Glossary

ancestors The people in a family who lived in earlier generations.

Buddha A spiritual leader in Asia who founded Buddhism, a religion followed today by people all over the world.

calligraphy The art of beautiful writing, usually done with a brush and ink.

chee goo 茨菇 The Chinese name for a vegetable called arrowroot eaten at the New Year in the belief that it will bring a family many sons.

Chinese calendar The lunar calendar.

Chinese character A pictograph representing a word in the Chinese language.

dahn sahn 蛋散 Cookies made from fried wonton covered with powdered sugar.

dragon A powerful, mythological animal said to bring good luck.

fai chun 揮春 Popular Chinese sayings that often consist of four characters.

fat choy 髮菜 A black, hair-like moss used in Chinese cooking and a symbol of prosperity.

fook 福 A Chinese character meaning "good luck."

Gregorian calendar A system of measuring time in which the length of a month is determined by the movement of the earth around the sun.

gung hay fat choy 恭喜發財 Chinese New Year's greeting that means "May you prosper."

jai 齋 A Chinese dish made up of a variety of vegetables, eaten at the New Year to purify the body.

lai see 利是 Bright red envelopes with a message on the front, containing a gift of money and given to children and unmarried adults during the Chinese New Year celebration.

Lion Dance A dance performed by members of a martial arts club to bring good luck to a home or a place of business.

lotus root The root of the lotus plant used in Chinese cooking.

lunar calendar A calendar that measures time by the movement of the moon.

Lunar New Year Another name for Chinese New Year, determined according to a lunar calendar.

martial arts The art of combat.

pomelo A large, yellow citrus fruit similar to a grape-fruit.

prosperity Good fortune and success.

purify To clean.

scroll A long, narrow piece of paper or fabric on which something is written or painted. The work is usually hung on a wall or rolled up on two sticks of wood.

wok A deep-sided pan used in many types of Chinese cooking.

Index

Page numbers in italic type indicate illustrations.